IRISH
GRAVESTONE INSCRIPTIONS

A Guide to Sources in Ulster

HERITAGE WORLD

- *Discover the path to your Irish roots* -

Heritage World is one of Ireland's foremost genealogy research companies, and caters for all family history requirements. If you have ancestral links with Ireland, we will assist you in discovering the path to your Irish roots. With over10 million computerised records, and researchers in Belfast and Dublin, we offer a fast, efficient and reasonably priced service to our clients. We are a member of both the Irish Family History Foundation and the Irish Genealogy Project and will undertake ancestral research for any county in Ireland.

In addition to research, we offer a full range of customised heritage products including family coats of arms, keyrings, name scrolls, personalised notepaper and publications on aspects of Irish history, folklore and culture. For any further information, please contact our Manager.

Heritage World Family History Services,
The Heritage Centre, 26 Market Square, Dungannon,
Co. Tyrone, Northern Ireland BT70 1AB
Tel. 01868-724187; Fax. 01868-752141.
e. mail: irishwld@iol.ie WEB SITE:- http://www.iol.ie./irishworld

IRISH GRAVESTONE INSCRIPTIONS

A GUIDE TO SOURCES IN ULSTER

William O'Kane & Eoin Kerr, Editors

Wilfred Halahakoon & Rosemary Nugent
Formatting and Tabulation

Genealogical Publishing Co., Inc.
and
Heritage World

Library of Congress Catalogue Card Number 99-71549
International Standard Book Number 0-8063-1616-0
Made in the United States of America

Cover illustration: Paul Donaghy

HERITAGE WORLD SURVEY OF GRAVESTONE INSCRIPTIONS

Heritage World has surveyed the gravestone inscriptions for almost nine hundred cemeteries across the northern part of Ireland. The great majority of these are located in Northern Ireland, although the figure includes a substantial number from two other Ulster counties, Donegal and Monaghan, as well as several from County Louth. The survey encompasses cemeteries of all religious denominations as well as those administered by local district and borough councils. In each case, there is an exact transcript of all gravestone inscriptions, together with a simple plan of the cemetery.

The importance of gravestone inscriptions

In addition to complementing other sources of genealogical data, the survey of gravestone inscriptions constitutes a valuable resource in its own right. In the same way as birth, marriage or death records, gravestone inscriptions are an important link with our ancestors. They often provide additional or incidental information - for instance on family relationships, occupations or place of residence - that may not be accessible via what we might call the 'official' civil or church records. Indeed, in those cases where no other written documentation is available, a gravestone inscription may be the only tangible link with a forebear. In a sense, too, every graveyard is a repository of local history, commemorating the names and achievements of a community. As such, they are of immense value to social historians and folklorists, as well as to genealogists, students and teachers.

A permanent record

Gravestones are durable, although centuries of weathering, erosion, vandalism and well-intentioned removal do take their toll. Inscriptions become fainter with time, and as the stone deteriorates there may well be no legible record left to posterity. By collating the information contained on gravestones and transferring it to computer, Heritage World has ensured that valuable data is retained for the use of present and future generations who might wish to discover the path to their roots.

Making data available

Up to now, gravestone inscriptions data has been used by Heritage World for its own research, but in response to requests from clients worldwide the material is now available to the general public. Information can be acquired either as an index, giving county, parish, person and cemetery names, date of death and denomination, or as a full gravestone inscription. These details can be supplied for any name in a particular cemetery, parish or county. Anyone wishing details of costs and availability should contact Heritage World at 26 Market Square, Dungannon, Co Tyrone, N. Ireland BT70 1AB; Tel 01868-724187, Fax 01868-752141.

About this book

This book lists all the cemeteries surveyed to date by Heritage World. There is a section for each county, with civil parishes listed alphabetically. All cemeteries within a civil parish are listed, together with their denomination. (See sample layout below.) For purposes of abbreviation, the various denominations are denoted as follows:-
RC = Roman Catholic
CI = Church of Ireland
PB = Presbyterian (including Reformed Presbyterian, Free Presbyterian and Non-Subscribing Presbyterian)
MOR = Moravian
METH = Methodist
BAPT = Baptist
CON = Congregational

QKR = Quaker
INTER = Interdenominational (including municipal)
In cases where there is no discernible denomination, for instance 'gospel hall', no designation is given. Obviously, the more someone knows about where their ancestor resided or is buried, or their religion, it will be easier to obtain relevant information. In many cases, only the name of the cemetery name is given, eg. 'St John'. However, most churches (and their adjoining cemeteries) are known by the name of the locality as well, eg. 'St John, Glenarm'. In such cases, this information is included on the basis that the more detail that is available, the better.

Parish	Cemetery	Denomination
Donaghmore	St Patrick	RC
Donaghmore	Garvagh Independent	PB
Donaghmore	St Michael, Castlecaulfield	CI
Donaghmore	First Carland	PB

Sample layout

Continuing the survey
Work is still proceeding on the gravestone inscriptions survey, although the great majority of cemeteries within Ulster have now been completed. Heritage World feels that, as it stands, this survey represents a substantial resource for anyone interested in furthering their research into Irish genealogy. As further cemeteries are added to our data base, the index will be updated. However, if at any time someone wishes to find out whether a particular cemetery not listed here is available, please contact Heritage World at the above address.

Willie O'Kane

Ireland - provinces, counties and chief towns

COUNTY ANTRIM

Antrim (from Irish *Andruim*, the habitation upon the waters) covers 1190 sq. miles and shares many physical and cultural features with western Scotland, 20 miles across the North Channel. Middle Stone Age peoples arrived here 7, 000 years ago, and their descendants became farmers, clearing woodland and fashioning tools. Late Stone Age peoples had a thriving business producing axe heads from the porcellanite rock of Rathlin Island and Tievebulliagh Mountain. As centuries passed, there was increasing commerce across the North Channel, with western Scotland and north eastern Ireland comprising one cultural and trading bloc.

Occasional rivalry produced war as when, in the 14th century, Edward Bruce invaded Ireland. Gaelic chieftains like O'Neill, McDonnell and O'Cahan supported the Scots against the English, and many Irish chieftains employed Scottish galloglasses, many of whom remained in Ireland.

With the defeat of Gaelic Ireland, the early 17th century Plantation of Ulster saw an influx of settlers from southern Scotland and northern England, and today the legacy of this Scottish immigration lives on in the surnames, religious affiliations, folk customs and dialect. Many Antrim surnames reflect the heritage of Scots and English settlers who have for nearly four centuries lived here. The five commonest - Smith, Johnston, Stewart, Wilson and Thompson - are of Scots or English origin, while Campbell, Moore, Millar, Hamilton and Boyd are similarly derived. Since their ancestors settled the best lands, many of these names are found in agriculture or its ancillary activities, while others were part of Ulster's thriving flax and linen industry of the 18th and 19th centuries. Most names of Scots descent are Protestant, while in the Glens of Antrim, stretching from Fair Head south to Ballygally, are found mostly descendants of Gaelic Irish and Highland Scots clans, with names like McAuley, McKillop, McSparran, McNaughton and McAllister. This area was not favoured by incoming settlers owing to its isolation and steep, inaccessible land. As such, the Glens

Antrim's 30m. Round Tower, dating from the 10th century

remained a repository of traditional Irish ways, and was largely Gaelic speaking up to early this century. The blend of natural woodlands, waterfalls and secluded valleys combine with mountain slopes, majestic headlands and quiet bays to form one of Ireland's loveliest regions.

Apart from Belfast, much of which is in Antrim, the chief towns of the county are Larne, Ballycastle, Glengormley, Ballymena, Lisburn, Carrickfergus, Templepatrick, Cushendall and Antrim town.

The Antrim Coast Road is one of the most scenic routes in Ireland. This famous limestone arch is near the village of Glenarm, north of Larne.

Civil Parish	Cemetery	Denomination
Aghagallon	St Patrick	RC
Aghalee	Aghalee Old	Inter
Ahoghill	St Colmanell	CI
Antrim	Friends	Qkr
Ardclinis	Ss. Patrick and Brigid	RC
Ardclinis	Nappin	Inter
Ardclinis	St Mary	CI
Ardclinis	St Mary, Star of the Sea	RC
Ardclinis	St John, Carnlough	RC
Ardclinis	Diskirt	RC
Armoy	Armoy	PB
Armoy	St Olcan	RC
Armoy	St Patrick	CI
Ballintoy	Ballintoy	CI
Ballintoy	Ss Mary and Joseph	RC
Ballintoy	Mosside	PB
Ballintoy	St Mary, Ballinlea	RC
Ballintoy	Toberkeigh	PB
Ballyclug	St Patrick, Crebilly	RC
Ballymoney	Ballymoney Municipal	Inter
Ballymoney	Our Lady and St Patrick	RC
Ballymoney	St Patrick	CI
Ballywillan	Ballywillan & Ballywillan Old	PB
Belfast	City Cemetery	Inter
Belfast	Balmoral Friends	Qkr
Belfast	Balmoral	Inter
Belfast	Hannahstown	RC
Belfast	Friars Bush	Inter
Belfast	Clifton Street	Inter
Belfast	Milltown	RC

Parish	Cemetery	Denomination
Belfast	St George	CI
Belfast	Christ Church	CI
Billy	Billy (Old, Middle and New)	CI
Billy	Dunseverick	CI
Carncastle	St Patrick	CI
Carnmoney	St Mary, Greencastle	RC
Carrickfergus	St Nicholas	CI
Carrickfergus	Templecorran	Inter
Carrickfergus	Kilroot	RC
Connor	Ballee (New)	CI
Culfeightrin	Cushendun	CI
Culfeightrin	Culfeightrin	CI
Culfeightrin	St Patrick, Cushendun	RC
Culfeightrin	St Patrick	RC
Culfeightrin	Cloughmills Ref. Presbyterian	PB
Culfeightrin	Bonamargy Friary	Inter
Derrykeighan	Dervock Presbyterian	PB
Derrykeighan	Gracehill	Mor
Derrykeighan	St Colman (Old)	CI
Derrykeighan	Toberdoney	PB
Drummaul	Randalstown (Old)	PB
Drummaul	First Randalstown	PB
Drummaul	St McNissi	RC
Dunaghy	St Mary, Glenravel	RC
Duneane	Our Lady of Lourdes, Moneyglass	RC
Finvoy	Finvoy Presbyterian	PB
Finvoy	Finvoy	CI
Glynn	Glynn	Inter
Grange of Drumtullagh	Drumtullagh	CI
Islandmagee	Glen	Inter

Parish	Cemetery	Denomination
Islandmagee	Raloo (Old)	Inter
Killagan	Killagan	RC
Killagan	Sacred Heart, Cloughmills	RC
Killagan	St Cuthbert, Bushmills	RC
Kildollagh	Kildollagh (Old)	CI
Kilraughts	Bushvale	PB
Kilraughts	First Kilraughts	PB
Kilraughts	Kilraughts (Old)	CI
Kilraughts	Kilraughts Reformed	PB
Kirkinriola	Kellswater Reformed	PB
Kirkinriola	St Patrick, Ballymarlow	CI
Kirkinriola	Ballymena (Old)	Inter
Larne	McGarel	Inter
Larne	St Cedma	CI
Layde	Layde (Old)	Inter
Layde	Cushendall	CI
Layde	St Mary, Cushendall	RC
Loughguile	St McNissi	RC
Loughguile	Ballyweaney	PB
Loughguile	St Patrick	RC
Loughguile	Lissanure Estate	Inter
Loughguile	All Saints	CI
Racavan	Skerry, Broughshane	CI
Racavan	St Patrick, Broughshane	CI
Racavan	Second Broughshane	PB
Racavan	Racavan	CI
Raloo	Ballygowan	RC
Raloo	Raloo	CI
Ramoan	St James, Ballycastle (Old)	CI
Ramoan	Ballycastle Gospel Hall	-

Civil Parish	Cemetery	Denomination
Romoan	Ramoan	PB
Ramoan	Ramoan (Old)	Inter
Ramoan	Holy Trinity	CI
Ramoan	Ballycastle Presbyterian	PB
Ramoan	Ss Patrick & Brigid, Ballycastle	RC
Ramoan	St James	CI
Rasharkin	Rasharkin	PB
Rathlin	St Thomas	Inter
Shankill	Shankill	Inter
Skerry	St Patrick, Braid	RC
Templepatrick	Mallusk (Old)	Inter
Tickmacrevan	St Patrick, Glenarm	CI
Tickmacrevan	St Mary, Glenarm	RC

COUNTY ARMAGH

At 435 sq. miles, Armagh is the smallest of Ulster's nine counties. Bounded by Down, Louth, Monaghan and Tyrone, it has a narrow shoreline at the head of Carlingford Lough. Known widely as the orchard county, Armagh has a high proportion of fertile land, and has always figured highly in the tortuous history of Ireland. Rich in pre-Christian sites and folklore, for the past fifteen hundred years Armagh has also been the seat of Christianity in Ireland.

The main towns are Armagh, Portadown, Lurgan, Markethill, Keady, Newtownhamilton and Tandragee. Farmland predominates in the north and centre, while the south

is more scenically varied with the Slieve Gullion range providing a backdrop of small hills interspersed with forests. Armagh was a centre of the linen industry for many generations, and the county was generally prosperous until the decline of linen. The late 18th century saw the formation of partisan groups like the White Boys, Hearts of Oak, Defenders and the Orange Order, when north Armagh emerged as a cockpit of many of the problems still besetting Ireland.

The name Armagh is from *Ard Macha* (Macha's Height) after Queen Macha who reputedly built a fortress on the hill now occupied by Armagh city. The adjacent Navan Fort was the royal capital of the kings of Ulster. Saint Patrick built his

Armagh's Church of Ireland Cathedral

first church here in the 5th century, and the settlement grew in importance to become the ecclesiastical capital of Ireland. Brian Boru is reputed to have been buried here in 1014, a measure of the importance of the site. Armagh city offers cultural and scientific attractions, with some of Ireland's finest Georgian architecture, a world-famous planetarium and fine public library - a legacy of the far-sighted and liberal 18th century Protestant Primate, Archbishop Robinson.

Armagh featured in the long campaign by Gaelic Ireland to resist English encroachment, and at the battle of Yellow Ford in 1598 Hugh O'Neill inflicted the worst ever defeat on the English in Ireland. In 1646, Hugh's nephew, Owen Roe O'Neill, carried on this tradition by defeating a combined Scots and English army at the Battle of Benburb. The Ulster Plantation saw the expulsion of native families like O'Neills, O'Hanlons and McCahans, and their lands divided amongst mainly English settlers and some from Scotland. The principal names of the county comprise an equitable mix of native Irish and settler families, and include Murphy, O'Hare, O'Hanlon, Hughes, Wilson, Campbell, Watson and Thompson.

Armagh's Roman Catholic Cathedral, built in the late 19th century

Civil Parish	Cemetery	Denomination
Aghaderg	St Mary, Lisnagade	RC
Armagh	Bullys Acre	Inter
Armagh	Sandy Hill	RC
Armagh	St Catherine Convent	RC
Armagh	St Mark, Armagh	CI
Ballymore	Poyntzpass	PB
Ballymore	Relicarn	RC
Ballymore	St Coleman, Clare	RC
Ballymore	St Mary, Acton	CI
Ballymoyer	Whitecross (Old)	Inter
Ballymoyer	Kingsmills	PB
Ballymoyer	St Luke, Whitecross	CI
Ballyure	St Malachy	RC
Clonallan	St Patrick, Mayobridge	RC
Clonfeacle	Legar Hill	CI
Clonfeacle	St Jarlath (Old)	RC
Clonfeacle	St Jarlath (New)	RC
Creggan	Creggan	CI
Creggan	Freeduff, Cullyhanna	PB
Creggan Lower	St Patrick, Cullyhanna	RC
Derrynoose	Sacred Heart, Lislea	RC
Derrynoose	St John, Madden	CI
Derrynoose	St Joseph, Madden	RC
Donaghcloney	Waringstown	PB
Dromore	St Coleman, Dromore	RC
Drumcree	Church of Ascension, Drumcree	CI
Drumcree	St Patrick, Garvaghey Rd.	RC
Drumgath	Immac Concept, Lissummon	RC
Eglish	Immac Concept, Tullysara	RC
Forkhill	Forkhill	CI

Civil Parish	Cemetery	Denomination
Forkhill	St Patrick, Urnai	RC
Jonesborough	Jonesborough	CI
Jonesborough	Sacred Heart	RC
Keady	Ballymacnab (Old), Tassagh	RC
Keady	St Mary, Granemore (Old)	RC
Keady	St Mary Granemore (New)	RC
Keady	St Matthew, Keady	CI
Keady	St Mochua	RC
Keady	St Patrick	RC
Keady	Tassagh (Old)	Inter
Kilclooney	Ballymacnab (Old)	RC
Kilclooney	St Michael, Claudymore	RC
Kildarton	Drumminis	PB
Kildarton	Kildarton	CI
Kildarton	Kildarton	CI
Killevy	Bessbrook	Meth
Killevy	Bessbrook	PB
Killevy	Church Rock, Camlough	CI
Killevy	Convent of Mercy, Bessbrook	RC
Killevy	Craigmore	PB
Killevy	Killevy	RC
Killevy	Killevy (Old)	RC
Killevy	Meigh	CI
Killevy	Mullaghglass	CI
Killevy	Mullaghglass (New)	CI
Killevy	Sacred Heart, Cloghogue	RC
Killevy	Soc of Friends, Bessbrook	Qkr
Killevy	Ss Peter and Paul, Bessbrook	RC
Killevy	St Joseph, Meigh	RC
Killevy	St Luke	CI

Civil Parish	Cemetery	Denomination
Killevy	St Malachy, Camlough	RC
Killevy	St Michael, Killeen	RC
Kilmore	Friends Meeting House	Qkr
Kilmore	Immac Concept, Mullavilly	RC
Kilmore	Moneys	Meth
Kilmore	Richill	PB
Kilmore	St Aidan	CI
Kilmore	St Aidan, Salters Grange	CI
Kilmore	Vinecash	PB
Leady	St Joseph, Madden	RC
Lisnadill	Ballinabeck, Tandragee	Meth
Lisnadill	Red Barns	PB
Lisnadill	Redrock	PB
Lisnadill	St John	CI
Lisnadill	St Mark	CI
Lisnadill	Tandragee	PB
Loughgall	Loughgall	Inter
Loughgall	Loughgall	PB
Loughgall	Loughgall	PB
Loughgall	St Patrick	RC
Loughgall	St Patrick, Loughgall	RC
Loughgall	St Peter, Collegeland	RC
Loughgilly	Belleek	CI
Loughgilly	St Lawrence O'Toole	RC
Loughgilly	St Malachy, Ballymoyer	RC
Lurgan	Aghagallon (Old)	Inter
Magheralin	Holy Trinity	CI
Montiaghs	St Patrick, Derrymacash	RC
Mullaghbrack	Mullaghbawn	RC
Mullaghbrack	St James	RC

Civil Parish	Cemetery	Denomination
Mullaghbrack	St John	CI
Mullaghbrack	St John, Markethill	CI
Mullavilly	Immac Concept	RC
Newry	Tremont (Old), Lisserboy	CI
Seagoe	Seagoe Municipal	Inter
Seagoe	St Gobhan	CI
Seagoe	St Saviour, Portadown	CI
Shankill	Dougher	RC
Shankill	Kernan	Inter
Shankill	Lurgan Quaker	Qkr
Shankill	Lynastown Friends	Qkr
Shankill	Sacred Heart Convent	RC
Shankill	St Coleman	RC
Shankill	St John Evangelist	RC
Tartaraghan	St John	RC
Tynan	Middletown	PB
Tynan	St Andrew, Middletown	CI
Tynan	St John, Middletown	RC
Tynan	St Joseph	RC
Tynan	St Joseph Convent	RC
Tynan	St Vindic	CI

COUNTY DERRY-LONDONDERRY

The modern county of Derry (or Londonderry, as it was designated by the terms of the settlement under King James 1st) was created in 1613 out of what had been known for centuries as the county of Coleraine, together with sections of the territory of the Earl of Tyrone (Hugh O'Neill) south of the Sperrins, and the district of Cianachta (Keenaught) along the valley of the River Roe. Half the land in the new county was shared out among a number of London companies for the purpose of settlement. Although some arrangements were made with a few of the native chieftains, by and large their land was forfeit - as a result of what was adjudged their treasonable behaviour in resisting conquest.

Derry is the anglicised form of *Doire*, (place of the oaks, or oakwood), and covers an area of 810 sq. miles. Prior to the Plantation, great wooded fastnesses and expanses of bleak upland covered large tracts of Tyrone and Derry, hindering the English advance. The forest of Glenkonkeine stretched from Tyrone into Derry and along the flanks of the Sperrin mountains, and legend has it that a man could travel from Dungannon to Derry from tree to tree, never touching the ground. But the war of attrition and mass destruction of livestock and crops wore down the Gaelic clans, and their eventual defeat and

dispossession set the scene for the Plantation of Ulster.

The Inishowen peninsula of Donegal is, in a sense, a northern extension of Derry, and the thrust of social and economic identification on the peninsula has always been south towards the Foyle lowlands. North Derry has a high incidence of the names associated with Donegal, such as O'Doherty, Gormley, Friel, McLaughlin, McGilligan, Mullan, Gallagher and Coyle. Other principal names are O'Kane and McCloskey, whose ancestral O'Cahan chiefs were key allies of O'Neill up to the 17th century.

Derry has some of the most fertile and productive land in Ireland, with Limavady and the reclaimed foreshores of Lough Foyle famed for high quality early potatoes. The chief rivers are the Foyle, rising in the Sperrins; the Bann, which forms the eastern boundary with Antrim; the Roe; the Faughan and the Moyola. Derry city is the largest town, with Coleraine, Limavady, Magherafelt, Draperstown and Portstewart among the others. In the late 1960s Derry saw the earliest civil rights marches, which set in train events leading to decades of severe political unrest in Northern Ireland. As for the matter of the county's name, most Nationalists call it Derry and most Unionists Londonderry - with the politically correct preferring Derry-Londonderry. This latter term manages simultaneously to please or displease half the population, depending on one's viewpoint.

Bishop's Gate, Derry City, erected in 1789

Civil Parish	Cemetery	Denomination
Aghadowey	First Aghadowey	PB
Aghadowey	Augherton (Old)	Inter
Aghadowey	St Guaire	CI
Aghanloo	Derramore	PB
Aghanloo	St Geddan	CI
Arboe	Ss Joseph and Malachy	RC
Artrea	St Patrick, Loup	RC
Ballinderry	St John, Ballyronan	CI
Ballyscullion	Church Island, Loughbeg	RC
Ballyscullion	St Mary, Bellaghy	RC
Ballyscullion	St Tida, Bellaghy	CI
Balteagh	Balteagh	PB
Balteagh	Balteagh (Old and New)	CI
Balteagh	St Matthew, Drumsurn	RC
Banagher	Banagher	CI
Banagher	St Joseph, Feeny	RC
Banagher	St Mary, Altinure	RC
Boveagh	Ss Peter and Paul, Ballymonie	RC
Boveagh	St Eugenius	RC
Clondermot	Altnagelvin	Inter
Clondermot	Glendermot	CI
Clondermot	Glendermot	PB
Clondermot	St Mary, Ardmore (Old and New)	RC
Clondermot	Glendermot	CI
Coleraine	Coleraine	Inter
Coleraine	Dromore	PB
Coleraine	St John	RC
Coleraine	St John, Strand Road	CI
Coleraine	St Patrick	CI
Coleraine	St Paul, Killdollagh (Old)	CI

Civil Parish	Cemetery	Denomination
Cumber Lower	Holy Trinity	CI
Cumber Upper	St Conestan, Straidarren	CI
Cumber Upper	St Patrick, Claudy	RC
Desertegny	Linsfort	CI
Desertlyn	Ss John and Trea, Moneymore	RC
Desertmartin	Boveagh	PB
Desertmartin	St Conghall	CI
Desertmartin	St Mary, Coolcam	RC
Desertoghill	St Eugene, Craigavole	RC
Drumachose	Drenagh	CI
Drumachose	Drumachose	PB
Drumachose	First Limavady	PB
Drumachose	Whitehill	Inter
Dunboe	Castlerock (Old and New)	PB
Dunboe	First Dunboe	PB
Dunboe	Second Dunboe	PB
Dunboe	Formoyle	CI
Dunboe	St Mary, Castlerock	RC
Dunboe	St Paul, Dunboe	CI
Dungiven	Dungiven (Old)	Inter
Dungiven	Gelvin (Old)	RC
Dungiven	St Patrick	RC
Errigal	First Garvagh (Old and New)	PB
Errigal	St Joseph, Glenullin	RC
Errigal	St Mary, Ballerin	RC
Errigal	St Paul, Garvagh	CI
Faughanvale	Faughanvale	PB
Faughanvale	St Canice, Eglinton	CI
Faughanvale	Star of the Sea	RC
Faughanvale	Tamnaherin	RC

Civil Parish	Cemetery	Denomination
Kilcronaghan	Kilcronaghan	CI
Killelagh	Granaghan (Old)	RC
Killelagh	St John, Granaghan	RC
Kilrea	Our Lady of Assumption	RC
Macosquin	Ballylintagh (Old)	PB
Macosquin	Christ Church, Limavady	CI
Macosquin	Crossgar	PB
Macosquin	Macosquin	PB
Macosquin	St Mary, Limavady	RC
Macosquin	St Mary, Macosquin	CI
Maghera	Culnady Presbyterian	PB
Maghera	St Lurach, Maghera	CI
Maghera	St Patrick, Glen	RC
Magherafelt	Christ Church	CI
Magherafelt	Milltown	RC
Magherafelt	St Trea, Newbridge	RC
Tamlaght	Tamlaght, Ballykelly	PB
Tamlaghtfinlagan	Ballykelly Presbyterian	CI
Tamlaghtfinlagan	Myroe	PB
Tamlaght O'Crilly	Drumagarner	RC
Tamlaghtard	Greystone Reformed Presbyterian	PB
Tamlaghtard	Magilligan	PB
Tamlaghtard	St Aidan, Magilligan	RC
Tamlaghtard	St Cadan, Duncrun	CI
Tamlaghtard	St Canice	RC
Templemore	Derry City Cemetery	Inter
Templemore	Holy Trinity, Culmore	CI
Templemore	St Augustine	CI
Templemore	St Columb Cathedral	CI
Templemore	St Columba. Long Tower	RC

COUNTY DONEGAL

Ulster's largest county covers 1,820 sq. miles and has one of the longest coastlines in Ireland. The name comes from *Dun na nGall*, (fort of the foreigners), and the Inishowen peninsula in north Donegal was associated with septs of the Cineal Eoghain from whom most native Ulster names derive. The remarkable stone fortress, Grianian of Aileach, atop a hill overlooking Lough Swilly is a testament to their power. Over several centuries various septs spread out south and east, with the O'Neills and McLaughlins competing for supremacy. In the Ulster Plantation, east Donegal was extensively settled by Scots, whose descendants bear names like Johnston, Cunningham, Patton and McLean. The west remained the rugged and impoverished preserve of dispossessed native Irish families like the Gallaghers, Dohertys, O'Boyles and Sweeneys.

In the Great Famine of 1846-48 west Donegal was one of the worst affected areas, and succeeding generations witnessed high levels of emigration. In terms of scenic variety and landscapes, north and west Donegal rank among the most beautiful anywhere, with a wealth of mountains and valleys, dramatic cliffs and beautiful uncrowded beaches. Errigal, Muckish, and Slieve Snaght offer superb hill-walking, while the sea-cliffs of Slieve League are the highest in Europe. Off-shore islands of

Tory and Arranmore offer a unique mix of traditional lifestyle and unspoiled landscape. Its geographical isolation helped preserve in Donegal remnants of the traditional Gaelic culture that had characterised most of Ulster for centuries. The Irish language is still spoken in several Gaeltacht regions of the west, while in many communities there flourishes a rich aural folk history. Irish painter Derek Hill has commemorated the Gaeltacht landscapes and faces in his portraits of Donegal life which are housed in the Glebe Gallery near Churchill.

Monument to the Four Masters, Donegal Town

The chief town is Letterkenny, a busy centre of light industry and education at the head of Lough Swilly, with Ballyshannon, Buncrana, Killybegs, Moville, Ballybofey, Donegal and Dunfanaghy among the other notable centres of population. The small town of Kincasslagh is famous on two counts; it is close to Donegal's only airport, and is also the home of singer Daniel O'Donnell whose sentimental ballads have proved a resounding success throughout Ireland and parts of Scotland and England. Donegal town is where the Annals of the Four Masters were compiled in the 1630s. This is a history of Ireland from earliest times and is an invaluable source of information much valued by historians. A 25 foot high monument in the town square commemorates their achievement.

Civil Parish	Cemetery	Denomination
All Saints	St Blaithin, St Johnston	RC
All Saints	St Johnston Presbyterian	PB
Burt	St Aengus	RC
Clonleigh	Clonleigh, Lifford (Old)	RC
Donaghmore	St Mary, Castlefin	RC
Fahan	St Mura	RC
Fahan	St Mura	CI
Inch	Inch	Inter
Inch	Inch	CI
Inch	Inch	PB
Inch	Our Lady of Lourdes	RC
Inshowen	St Eigne	RC
Muff	Sacred Heart	RC
Muff	St Patrick, Iskaheen	RC
Tamlaght Finlagan	St Finlough, Glack	RC
Tamlaght Finlagan	Tamlaght Finlagan	CI
Tamlaght Finlagan	Largy	PB
Tamlaghtard	Salvin	RC
Urney	St Columba	RC
Urney	St Eugene	RC

COUNTY DOWN

County Down (*An Dun*, the fort) occupies just over 955 square miles, with the north having the best agricultural land, and the south dominated by the Mourne mountains. Strangford Lough, an inlet of the Irish Sea, creates the Ards Peninsula, an area of rolling dairy farms and sandy beaches, threaded by small country roads. Drowned drumlins form small islands along the lough shore, and its sheltered location makes the lough a haven of bird life. In the south, Carlingford Lough separates Down from County Louth.

The Mournes provide a variety of mountain scenery unmatched in Ireland. Slieve Donard (2,796 ft.) is the highest peak in Ulster, and within a radius of a few miles are a dozen summits above 2,000 feet. Tourism is an important component of Down's economy and Newcastle, at the foot of Slieve Donard, is one of the county's main towns. Farther north are Bangor, a popular seaside destination for nearby Belfast, and quieter coastal villages like Donaghadee and Strangford. Other towns are Newtownards, Downpatrick, Banbridge, Comber, Ballynahinch, Hillsborough, Castlewellan, Rathfriland, Dromore and Newry.

In ancient times, Down was part of the kingdom of the Ulaid, from which the name Ulster is derived, and in early Christian

times, the Ui Neill dynasty emerged as the dominant grouping in Ulster, producing the various branches that give us native names like McGuiness, O'Neill and McCartan. Down's proximity to the Scottish and English coasts resulted in commercial and social intercourse long before the 17th century. Names like Savage and White are quite common, their origins going back to Anglo-Norman invasions of the 12th and 13th centuries. But the influx of Scots and English settlers in the early 17th century left the deepest imprint. Thompson and Smith are among the commonest names in Down today, as are Campbell and Patterson. This strong Scottish complexion is reflected in the rest of the county's roll call - Martin, Wilson, Graham, Johnston, Robinson, Hamilton, Bell and Boyd.

The older Irish names are mostly confined to the mountainous portion of the county, whence they were driven as a result of the systematic settlement schemes of the early 17th century. (Antrim and Down were not 'planted' in the sense that Derry, Tyrone, Donegal and Cavan were; the eastern counties proved attractive to incoming settlers and there was little in the way of organised resistance.)

In terms of architecture, agriculture, politics and industry, the county reflects its multi-faceted settlement history. The north's well tended farms and seaside villages are unmistakably British, while the kingdom of Mourne in the south has a stronger echo of Gaelic ways.

Church of Ireland Cathedral,
Downpatrick, County Down

Civil Parish	Cemetery	Denomination
Aghaderg	Loughbrickland	CI
Aghaderg	St John, Loughbrickland	RC
Aghaderg	St Mary, Ballyvarley	RC
Aghaderg	St Matthew	CI
Annahilt	Annahilt	CI
Annahilt	Annahilt	PB
Annahilt	Cargacreevy	PB
Annahilt	Loughaghery	PB
Annahilt	Loughaghery	PB
Ardglass	Ardglass	PB
Ardglass	St Nicholas, Ardglass	CI
Ardglass	St Nicholas, Ardglass	RC
Ballee	Ballee	CI
Ballee	Ballee Non-Sub	PB
Ballee	Ballycruttle	RC
Ballyculter	Ballyculter, Churchtown	CI
Ballyculter	Lough Inch	Inter
Ballyculter	Old Court, Strangford	CI
Ballyhalbert	Ballyhemli Non-Sub	PB
Ballykinler	St Patrick, Ballykinler (Old and New)	RC
Ballymore	Cremore, Poyntzpass	PB
Ballymore	Tyrone Ditches	PB
Ballyphilip	Ardquin	CI
Ballyphilip	Ballyphilip	CI
Ballyphilip	Ballytrustan, Portaferry	RC
Ballyphilip	Spa	PB
Ballyphilip	St Patrick, Ballyphilip	RC
Ballyphilip	Templecraney, Portaferry	CI
Bangor	St John, Lisbane	RC
Blaris	Maze	PB

Civil Parish	Cemetery	Denomination
Brigh	St Patrick, Legamady	RC
Bryansford	Kilcoo	CI
Clonallan	St Peter, Warrenpoint	RC
Clonallan	Clonallan, Warrenpoint	Inter
Clonallan	St Mary, Burren	RC
Clonduff	Hilltown	PB
Clonduff	St John Baptist	RC
Clonduff	St John Evangelist, Hilltown	RC
Clonduff	St John, Hilltown	CI
Comber	Comber Municipal	PB
Comber	Comber Non-Sub	PB
Comber	St Mary, Comber	CI
Comber	St Mary Comber	RC
Donaghdee	Carrowdore	CI
Donaghcloney	Blackscull	Meth
Donaghcloney	Donaghcloney	PB
Donaghcloney	Donaghcloney	PB
Donaghcloney	St Teresa, Tullybarn	RC
Donaghcloney	First Warrenpoint	PB
Donaghmore	St Bartholomew	CI
Down	Down Cathedral	RC
Down	Downpatrick	PB
Down	First Non-Sub, Downpatrick	PB
Down	Holy Trinity, Hollymount	CI
Down	St Margaret, Downpatrick	CI
Down	St Patrick, Downpatrick	RC
Down	Struell	Inter
Dromore	Dromore Non-Sub	PB
Drumballyroney	Drumballyroney	CI
Drumbeg	Kilcairn (Old)	RC

Civil Parish	Cemetery	Denomination
Drumbo	Immac Heart, Carryduff	RC
Drumbo	Bailies Mills Ref Pres	PB
Drumbo	Carryduff Presbyterian	PB
Drumgath	Drumgath	CI
Drumgath	Drumgath	RC
Drumgath	First Rathfriland	PB
Drumgath	Second Rathfriland	PB
Drumgath	Third Rathfriland	PB
Drumgath	Rathfriland Ref Pres	PB
Drumgath	St Coleman, Rathfriland	RC
Drumgath	St Mary, Rathfriland	RC
Drumgath	St Michael, Rathfriland	RC
Drumgooland	Benraw	PB
Drumgooland	Drumlee, Ballyard	PB
Dunsfort	St Mary, Dunsford	CI
Dunsfort	St Mary, Dunsford	RC
Hillsborough	Hillsborough	Inter
Hillsborough	Society of Friends, Hillsborough	Qkr
Hillsborough	Kilwarlin	CI
Hillsborough	Kilwarlin	RC
Hillsborough	Kilwarlin Moravian	Mor
Holywood	Old Priory, Holywood	Inter
Inch	Inch Abbey	CI
Inishargy	Balligan	CI
Kilbroney	Knotty Ash, Rostrevor	Inter
Kilbroney	Rostrevor (Old)	CI
Kilbroney	St Bronagh	RC
Kilclief	Kilclief	CI
Kilclief	St Malachy, Kilclief	RC
Kilclooney	St Patrick, Ballymacnab	RC

Civil Parish	Cemetery	Denomination
Kilcoo	Bryansford	CI
Kilcoo	Bryansford	RC
Kilcoo	Drumee, Newcastle	PB
Kilcoo	St Coleman, Newcastle (Old and New)	CI
Kilkoo	St Coleman, Newcastle	CI
Kilkoo	St Michael, Newcastle	RC
Kilkeel	Annalong Presbyterian	PB
Kilkeel	Christ Church	CI
Kilkeel	Kilhorne, Annalong	CI
Kilkeel	Kilkeel Baptist	Bapt
Kilkeel	Kilkeel Presbyterian	PB
Kilkeel	Kilkeel Free Pres	PB
Kilkeel	Kilkeel (Old)	CI
Kilkeel	Massforth	RC
Kilkeel	Moravian	Mor
Kilkeel	Mourne	PB
Killaney	First Boardmills	PB
Killaney	Second Boardmills	PB
Killaney	Killaney	PB
Killevy	First Drumbanagher, Jerretspass	PB
Killevy	First Jerretspass	PB
Killevy	St Mary, Barr	RC
Killevy	St Mary, Drumbanagher	RC
Killinchy	Ballygowan	PB
Killinchy	Ballygowan	RC
Killinchy	Ballygowan Free Pres	PB
Killinchy	Ballymacashen	PB
Killinchy	Killaresy (Old)	Inter
Killinchy	Killinchy Non-Sub	PB
Killinchy	Killinchy Presbyterian	PB

Civil Parish	Cemetery	Denomination
Killinchy	Raffery	PB
Killinchy	Ravara Non-Sub	PB
Killinchy	St Andrew, Killinchy	CI
Killinchy	St Joseph, Carrickmannon	RC
Killinchy	St Mary, Churchill	CI
Killyleagh	Killowen (Old)	Inter
Killyleagh	First Killyleagh	PB
Killyleagh	St John Evangelist	CI
Killyleagh	St Mary, Killeleagh	RC
Kilmegan	Aughlisnafin, Castlewellan	RC
Kilmegan	Dechomet, Castlewellan	RC
Kilmegan	Drumgooland	CI
Kilmegan	Drumgooland	PB
Kilmegan	St Mary, Castlewellan (Old)	RC
Kilmegan	St Paul, Castlewellan	CI
Kilmood	St Mary, Kilmood	CI
Kilmore	Ahory	PB
Kilmore	Christ Church, Crossgar	CI
Kilmore	Holy Family, Teeconnaught	RC
Kilmore	Kilmore (Old)	CI
Kilmore	Kilmore Pres, Crossgar	PB
Kilmore	Lissara, Crossgar	PB
Kilmore	Rademon Non-Sub, Crossgar	PB
Kilmore	Teeconnaught, Annacloy	RC
Knockbreda	Gilnahirk	PB
Loughanisland	Seaforde	CI
Loughanisland	St McCartan (Old and New)	RC
Loughanisland	St Mary of Angels, Drumaroad	RC
Magheradrool	Ballynahinch	Con
Magheradrool	First Ballynahinch	PB

Civil Parish	Cemetery	Denomination
Magheradrool	Cargycreevy	PB
Magheradrool	Edengrove	PB
Magheradrool	Magheradrool	Inter
Magheradrool	Magheradrool (Old)	Inter
Magheradrool	St John Baptist, Ballynahinch	RC
Magheradrool	St Patrick, Ballynahinch	RC
Magherahamlet	Magherahamlet	CI
Magherahamlet	Magherahamlet	PB
Magherally	Magherally	CI
Moira	Lurganville	RC
Newry	Convent of Mercy	RC
Newry	Glascar, Ballinaskeagh	PB
Newry	Meeting House Green (Old and New)	PB
Newry	Monks Hill, Newry	Inter
Newry	Mountkearney	Private
Newry	Poor Clare Convent	RC
Newry	Ryans, Finnard	PB
Newry	Ss Joseph and Coleman, Saul	RC
Newry	St Coleman, Shinn	RC
Newry	St Mary, Newry	RC
Newry	St Patrick, Newry	CI
Newry	Templegowran	Inter
Rathmullan	St Ann, Killough	CI
Rathmullan	St John, Rathmullan	CI
Rathmullan	St Mary, Rossglass	RC
Saintfield	Saintfield	CI
Saintfield	First Saintfield	PB
Saintfield	Second Saintfield	PB
Saul	St Patrick, Saul	CI
Saul	St Patrick, Saul	RC

Civil Parish	Cemetery	Denomination
Seapatrick	Ballydown	RC
Seapatrick	Banbridge	Inter
Seapatrick	Banbridge	RC
Seapatrick	Drumdonald, Banbridge	Inter
Seapatrick	Garvaghy, Banbridge	PB
Seapatrick	Lancastrian, Banbridge	PB
Seapatrick	St Patrick, Banbridge	Con
Seapatrick	Ballydown	PB
Seapatrick	Banbridge Non-Sub	PB
Seapatrick	First Banbridge	PB
Seapatrick	Scarva Street, Banbridge	PB
Seapatrick	Seapatrick	CI
Shankill	Shankill	Inter
Tullylish	Clare	RC
Tullylish	All Saints	CI
Tullylish	Moyallen Friends	Qkr
Tullylish	Newmills, Gilford	PB
Tullylish	St Coleman, Laurencetown	RC
Tullylish	Tullylish	PB
Tullynakill	Tullynakill	Inter
Tyrella	Tyrella	CI
Warrenpoint	Alexian Bros, Warrenpoint.	RC

COUNTY FERMANAGH

Fermanagh is Northern Ireland's most westerly county, and ten percent of its 713 sq. miles is water. Fishing and dairying predominate over arable farming, and the county presents a lush blend of lakes, rivers, grassland and wooded islands. The name Fermanagh comes from the Irish *Feor Magh Eanagh*, the country of the lakes, and this proximity of land and water is a pervasive feature of the county. There is a traditional saying that for half the year Lough Erne is in Fermanagh, while for the other half Fermanagh is in Lough Erne - an observation that is not very far off the mark.

Upper and Lower Lough Erne, threaded by the River Erne, dominate the centre of Fermanagh, extending more than 40 miles from northwest to southeast. Draining into the Erne basin are the Arney, Sillees, Tempo, Kesh, Ballinamallard and Swanlinbar rivers. Apart from the Erne lakes, there are Loughs Melvin, Navar and Upper and Lower Macnean. The Erne-Shannon Waterway links Enniskillen with Limerick, so opening a new age of boat travel through the lakes and canals of central Ireland. The highest point is Cuilcagh Mountain (2,195 feet), on the Cavan border, while the limestone knolls, jagged valleys and cliff faces of the Knockmore district have earned it comparison with Switzerland.

The main town is Enniskillen, built on an island on the Erne, and smaller towns include Irvinestown, Lisnaskea, Garrison, Belleek, Derrygonnelly, Belcoo, Ballinamallard, Newtownbutler, Tempo, Brookeborough and Maguiresbridge.

Fermanagh's abundant water facilitated early settlement, and Stone Age axes have been found around Lough Macnean in the southwest of the county. Later settlers brought farming skills and erected fine stone tombs. There are many early Christian relics; the round towers and high crosses of Devenish

Street scene, Enniskillen, Co Fermanagh

Island continuing the earlier tradition of carved heads on Boa Island. Viking raiders penetrated Lough Erne in the 9th century, returning at various times over the next century or so.

Maguire was long the chief sept in Fermanagh, and in the late 16th century were allies of O'Neill and O'Donnell in their campaign against the English. Defeat resulted in the demise of Maguire power, and Fermanagh was subsequently escheated to the crown and planted with Scots and English settlers. Examples of these names - Cole, Hamilton, Dunbar, Elliott, Wilson and Irvine - are still widely represented. The main names, though, are those of native Ulster origin, and include Maguire, McManus, Dolan, McGovern, Cassidy, Reilly, McElroy and Flanagan.

Civil Parish	Cemetery	Denomination
Aghadea	St Mary, Brookeborough (New)	RC
Aghalurcher	Aghalurcher, Lisnaskea	Inter
Aghalurcher	All Saints, Mullaghfad	CI
Aghalurcher	Christ Church, Maguiresbridge	CI
Aghalurcher	Holy Cross, Lisnaskea	RC
Aghalurcher	Holy Trinity, Castle Balfour	CI
Aghalurcher	Maguiresbridge	Meth
Aghalurcher	Maguiresbridge	PB
Aghalurcher	Sallaghy, Lisnaskea	CI
Aghalurcher	St Joseph, Cooneen	RC
Aghalurcher	St Mary, Maguiresbridge	RC
Aghalurcher	Tullynageeran	RC
Aghavea	Brookeborough (Old)	RC
Belleek	Keenaghan	RC
Belleek	Slavin	CI
Belleek	St Michael, Mulleek	RC
Belleek	St Patrick, Finner	RC
Boho	Boho	CI
Boho	Sacred Heart	RC
Cleenish	Ballinaleck	CI
Cleenish	Lisbellaw	CI
Cleenish	Lisbellaw	PB
Cleenish	Mullaghdun	RC
Cleenish	Tattygar	CI
Cleenish	Templenaffrin	RC
Clones	Magheraveely, Uttony	RC
Clones	St Mary, Aghadrumsee	CI
Clones	St Mary, Magherarny	RC
Clones	St Tiernach, Roslea	RC
Derrybrusk	St Michael, Derrybrusk	CI

Civil Parish	Cemetery	Denomination
Derryvullen	Derryvullen (Old)	Inter
Derryvullen	Irvinestown	RC
Derryvullen	Irvinestown (Old and New)	CI
Derryvullen	Killadeas	CI
Derryvullen	Lisnarick	CI
Derryvullen	Sacred Heart, Irvinestown	RC
Derryvullen	St Patrick, Castle-Archdale	CI
Derryvullen	St Tiernach, Tamlaght	CI
Devenish	Garrison	CI
Devenish	Garrison	RC
Devenish	Immac Concept, Monea	RC
Devenish	St Molaise, Monea	CI
Drumkeeran	Montiaghroe	RC
Drumkeeran	St Mary, Bannagh	RC
Drumkeeran	Tirwinny	Meth
Drumkeeran	Tubrid	CI
Drummully	Drumcrin	RC
Drummully	Drummully (Old)	Inter
Drummully	St Mary, Newtownbutler	CI
Enniskillen	Breandrum	Inter
Enniskillen	Cavanaleck	PB
Enniskillen	Enniskillen Convent	RC
Enniskillen	Holy Trinity, Garvary	CI
Enniskillen	Immac Concept, Tempo	RC
Enniskillen	St McCartan	CI
Enniskillen	Tempo	CI
Enniskillen	Tempo	PB
Galloon	Galloon Island	RC
Galloon	St Comgall, Galloon	CI
Galloon	St Mary, Newtownbutler	CI

Civil Parish	Cemetery	Denomination
Galloon	St Patrick, Donagh (Old)	RC
Inishmacsaint	Derrygonnelly	Inter
Inishmacsaint	St Patrick, Derrygonnelly	RC
Killesher	St Joan, Killesher	CI
Killesher	St Patrick, Killesher	RC
Kinawley	Callow Hill	Inter
Kinawley	Holy Trinity, Derrylin	CI
Kinawley	St Mary, Teemore	RC
Kinawley	St Ninnidh, Knockninny (Old & New)	RC
Magheracross	Magheracross (Old)	Inter
Magheracross	St Mary, Coa	RC
Magheracross	Sydare	Meth
Magheraculmon	Lack	CI
Magheraculmon	St Mary, Ardress	CI
Monaghan	St McCartan Cathedral	RC
Rossory	Rossory	CI
Rossory	Rossory (Old)	CI
Trory	St Michael, Trory	CI

COUNTY LOUTH

Louth, the most northerly county of Leinster, is also the smallest in Ireland, covering some 340 sq. miles. It is bounded in the north and west by Ulster, in the east by the Irish Sea and in the south the River Boyne marks the boundary with County Meath. Most of the land is of good quality, reflected in the rich and varied agricultural economy. The Cooley Peninsula, between Dundalk Bay and Carlingford Lough, offers beautiful rambling and climbing country. Carlingford Mountain is over 1,900 ft high and the range is interspersed with wooded valleys, while the village of Carlingford is among the most picturesque in Ireland. The ruins of the 13th century Castleroche, near the village of Louth, point to the power and influence of the Norman presence, while Mellifont Abbey is an important ecclesiastical site going back to the 12th century. Monasterboice is also associated with early Irish Christianity, possessing some of the finest High Crosses in the country. Other settlements of historic and scenic interest include Omeath, Ravensdale, Castlebellingham and Ardee.

The port of Dundalk for many centuries played an important role in trade and commerce along the east coast, and also commanded the approach to the Pass of

Moyry and Ulster Gap. Accordingly, it has witnessed many dynastic and territorial upheavals in its history. The town has an important maritime and manufacturing history, with brewing, leather and tobacco industries. Farther south is Drogheda, near the mouth of the Boyne and close to the impressive Stone Age monuments of Newgrange and Dowth. Drogheda has a rich architectural history, and was one of the main centres of the Pale in Anglo-Norman times. It was here that Poyning's Law was passed in 1495 stating that no law could be passed by the Irish parliament without approval from the English crown. The town was beseiged in the 1641 Rising, then in 1649 it was the scene of Cromwell's infamous massacre of large numbers of inhabitants. Many who survived were transported as slaves to the sugar plantations of Barbados.

Monasterboice High Cross, one of the finest in Ireland

Louth has a broad range of native Irish surnames with a mix of English and Welsh among them, reflecting the county's history. Among the most most common surnames are Byrne, Kelly, Murphy, Smith, Duffy and Clark.

St Mochta's House, in the village of Louth. Built around the 12th century, it commemorates the first Bishop of Louth, appointed by St Patrick himself.

Civil Parish	Cemetery	Denomination
Ballymascanlon	St Brigid, Kilcurry	RC
Carlingford	St Lawrence, Omeath	RC
Carlingford	St Michael, Carlingford	RC
Carlingford	Holy Trinity	RC
Dundalk	Dowdalshill	RC
Dundalk	Castletown	RC
Dundalk	Kanes (Old)	CI
Dundalk	Brid-A-Chrin	RC
Drumin	St Patrick, Drumintee	RC

COUNTY MONAGHAN

County Monaghan, comprising some 525 sq. miles, is a landlocked county having boundaries with four other Ulster counties - Tyrone, Armagh, Fermanagh and Cavan - as well as with Louth and Meath. The name derives from *Muineachan*, the place of the thickets. The landscape is a mix of rounded hills and poorly drained uplands, interspersed with more fertile soils on the lower parts where limestone predominates. The highest hills are the remote and featureless Slieve Beagh range in the northwest, along the Tyrone border, reaching around 1,200 feet. Other peaks are Cairmore, with its deep upland lake, and Crieve

Mountain overlooking the southern part of the county.

The Blackwater is the chief river, and today most of the county is given to pasture and beef farming, with sheep on the higher farmland and mushroom-growing in the north. Monaghan is the county town, being the episcopal seat of Clogher diocese and noted for St. Macartan's Roman Catholic cathedral. The town has long served a relatively prosperous mixed-farming area, and despite a decline in local industies over the past few decades, evidence of its former solidity remains in buildings like the Market House, dating from the 1790s, the Westenra Hotel and the nearby printing works producing the *Northern Standard* newspaper. Clones, 12 miles west of Monaghan, possesses a fine High Cross in the market place and several notable Georgian houses. The chief GAA playing field in Ulster is located here, and provincial matches regularly attract tens of thousands to the town. Castleblaney, at the head of Lough Mucknoo, one of the largest of Monaghan's many lakes, is the hometown of popular singer 'Big Tom' McBride. Other towns include Newbliss, Emyvale and Ballybay. Carrickmacross, in the southeast of the county, is noted for its fine lace, a tradition stretching back several centuries and today carried on by a dedicated co-operative movement. Near Carrickmacross is the hamlet of Inishkeen, near which Patrick Kavanagh (1904-67) was born in the townland of Mucker. His poetry, increasingly recognised as among the best of any Irish writer, celebrated the dignity of life amid the small farms and country people he knew so well. The principal family names of Monaghan are mainly of native Ulster origin, although in the Plantation many Scots and English settlers arrived in the county. In no particular numerical order they include: McMahon, McKenna, Hughes, McCabe, Smith, Kelly, Maguire, Murray, Woods, O'Connolly, Duffy, Leslie, Hamilton and Shirley.

The Market House, Monaghan, dating from 1792

Civil Parish	Cemetery	Denomination
Ballybay	Drumkeen	PB
Clones	St Mary, Clontibret	RC
Clones	Clough	RC
Clones	St McCartan, Aghadrumsee	RC
Clones	Smithborough	PB
Clontibret	St Michael, Annyalla	RC
Clontibret	All Saints, Doohamlet	RC
Donagh	Glennan	PB
Donagh	Drumbanagher	RC
Donagh	St Patrick, Corracrin	RC
Donagh	St Salvador, Glaslough	CI
Donagh	Glaslough	CI
Drumsnat	St Mary, Three Mile House	RC
Glennan	St Mary	RC
Kilmore	St Michael, Corcaghan	RC
Killevan	St Livinu, Killevan	RC
Monaghan	First Monaghan	PB
Monaghan	St McCartan Cathedral	RC
Monaghan	Old Cross, Monaghan	PB
Monaghan	Coolshannagh	Inter
Monaghan	Drumsnat	CI
Tehallan	St Patrick	RC
Tedavnet	St Dympna	RC
Tedavnet	St Mary, Urbleshanny	RC

COUNTY TYRONE

At 1,261 sq. miles, Tyrone is second in size only to Donegal in all of Ulster. It is a patchwork of barren mountain slopes and bogland, interspersed with winding river valleys and sandy lowlands where better soils and shelter have sustained agriculture and human settlement. The chief mountains, the Sperrins, run along the Derry border and from them descend the Mourne, Glenelly, Camowen and Owenkillew rivers, in whose valleys are found the towns of Omagh, Newtownstewart and Strabane. Higher up are Beragh, Sixmilecross, Carrickmore and Pomeroy, the highest town in Ulster.

There are many ancient graves, and a site near Cookstown has yielded the

oldest known Late Stone-Age house in the British Isles. Tyrone comes from *Tir Eoghain,* the land of Eoghain, a son of Niall of the Nine Hostages, whose descendants were the Cineal Eoghain, part of the northern Ui Neill, from which most native Ulster names derived. Among the most common names of native Ulster origin are O'Neill, Donnelly, Quinn, Kelly, McKenna, Devlin and McLaughlin.

The last O'Neill chieftain was Hugh, Earl of Tyrone (1550-1616), who led the final resistance by Gaelic Ireland against English forces. In 1607, with fellow chiefs and allies, he removed to Europe in the 'Flight of the Earls'. In the Plantation of Ulster his territory was planted with English and Scots settlers. Names like Stewart, Lindsay, Caulfield, Richardson and Cook appeared, and the towns of Omagh, Dungannon, Mountjoy, Clogher, Stewartstown, Newtownstewart and Cookstown were raised as monuments to their industry. Meanwhile, the dispossessed Gaelic people were pushed out to mountain slopes or marshy lough-shore. In 1641 Owen Roe and Phelim O'Neill, nephews of the great Hugh, led a campaign against the English that re-echoed the Elizabethan wars of the 1590s. In June 1646, Owen Roe defeated the army of General Robert Munroe near Benburb, inflicting over 3,000 casualties on the Scots.

Tyrone saw much emigration to the New World, where today there are sixteen towns called Tyrone. New Hampshire has a Stewartstown and Washington, Ohio and Iowa a Pomeroy each. Three presidents - James Buchanan (1857-1861), Ulysses S. Grant (1869-77) and Woodrow Wilson (1913-21) - had ancestral links with Tyrone.

Tyrone writers have long made their mark on Irish letters. William Carleton (1794-1869) was born in the Clogher Valley and his novels are a monument to Irish peasant life before the Great Famine. In more recent times, novelist Benedict Kiely, poet John Montague, satirist Flann O'Brien and playwright Brien Friel have all achieved world recognition.

Bell's Bridge, across the River Strule in Omagh, the chief town of Co. Tyrone.

Civil Parish	Cemetery	Denomination
Aghaloo	Aghaloo (Old)	Inter
Aghaloo	Minterburn	RC
Aghaloo	St Joseph, Caledon	RC
Aghaloo	St Mary, Aughnacloy	RC
Ardboe	Brookend	CI
Ardboe	Old Cross	CI
Ardboe	St Patrick	RC
Ardboe	St Peter, Moortown	RC
Ardstraw	Ardstraw	RC
Ardstraw	Baronscourt	CI
Ardstraw	Corrick	RC
Ardstraw	Douglas Bridge	PB
Ardstraw	Droit, Newtownstewart	PB
Ardstraw	Drumclamph	CI
Ardstraw	Drumlegagh	PB
Ardstraw	Magheracolton, Newtownstewart	Inter
Ardstraw	Pubble, Newtownstewart	RC
Ardstraw	St Eugene, Glenrock	RC
Ardstraw	St Eugene, Newtownstewart	CI
Artrea	St Patrick, Loup	RC
Aughintain	St Margaret, Clabby	CI
Ballinderry	Eglish, (Old)	CI
Ballinderry	St John, Ballinderry	CI
Ballyclog	Brigh	PB
Ballyclog	Ss Mary and Joseph, Coalisland	RC
Ballyclog	Ballyclog	Inter
Bodoney Lower	St Patrick, Gortin	RC
Bodoney Lower	Broughderg	CI
Bodoney Lower	St Mary, Rouskey (Old)	RC
Bodoney Lower	St Patrick, Gortin	RC

Civil Parish	Cemetery	Denomination
Bodoney Upper	Cranagh (Old)	RC
Bodoney Upper	Sacred Heart, Plumbridge	RC
Bodoney Upper	St Mary, Cranagh (New)	RC
Bodoney Upper	St Patrick, Greencastle	RC
Camus	Camus Monastery	RC
Camus	Convent of Mercy	RC
Camus	St Mary, Melmount	RC
Camus	St Patrick, Ballymagrory	CI
Camus	Strabane	Inter
Camus	Strabane, Patrick Street	Inter
Cappagh	Cappagh (Old)	CI
Cappagh	Cappagh (Old)	RC
Cappagh	Edenderry	CI
Cappagh	Edenderry	PB
Cappagh	Lislimnaghan	CI
Cappagh	Mountjoy	PB
Cappagh	St Mary, Killyclogher	RC
Cappagh	St Mary, Knockmoyle	RC
Carnteel	Ballyreagh	PB
Carnteel	Carnteel	Inter
Carnteel	Carnteel	PB
Carnteel	Glenhoy	PB
Carnteel	Knockconny	Bapt
Carnteel	St Brigid, Killens	RC
Clogher	Clogher	PB
Clogher	St Mark, Augher	CI
Clogher	St Mark, Newtownsaville	CI
Clogher	St McCartan	RC
Clogher	St McCartan, Augher	RC
Clogher	St Patrick	RC

Civil Parish	Cemetery	Denomination
Clogher	St Patrick, Eskra	RC
Clogherney	Immac Concept, Beragh	RC
Clogherney	Seskinore	PB
Clogherney	St Malachy, Seskinore	RC
Clonfeacle	Benburb Meeting House	PB
Clonfeacle	Eglish	PB
Clonfeacle	Grange Meeting House	Qkr
Clonfeacle	Holy Trinity, Brantry	CI
Clonfeacle	Holy Trinity, Drumsollen	CI
Clonfeacle	St Columba, Derrygortreevy	CI
Clonfeacle	St James	CI
Clonfeacle	St John, Moy	RC
Clonfeacle	St Patrick, Eglish (Old and New)	RC
Clonoe	St Brigid, Brocagh	RC
Clonoe	St Michael	CI
Clonoe	St Patrick, Clonoe	RC
Derryloran	Chapel Hill	RC
Derryloran	Cookstown Municipal	Inter
Derryloran	Forthill, Cookstown	Inter
Derryloran	St Luran	CI
Desertcreat	Desertcreat	CI
Desertcreat	Grange Reformed	PB
Desertcreat	Sacred Heart, Tullyodonnell	RC
Desertcreat	Sandholes	PB
Desertcreat	St John	RC
Desertcreat	St Mary, Rock	RC
Desertcreat	St Patrick	Inter
Donacavey	Castletown	CI
Donacavey	Donacavey (Old)	Inter
Donacavey	Fintona	Inter

Civil Parish	Cemetery	Denomination
Donacavey	Fintona	PB
Donacavey	Ss Peter and Paul, Fintona	RC
Donacavey	St Lawrence, Fintona	RC
Donaghedy	Donaghedy (Old)	Inter
Donaghedy	Grange	Inter
Donaghedy	Mountcastle, Donemana	Inter
Donaghedy	St James, Donemana	CI
Donaghedy	St John, Dunnalong	CI
Donaghedy	St Mary, Donemana	RC
Donaghedy	St Michael, Donemana	RC
Donaghedy	St Patrick, Donemana	RC
Donaghenry	Brackaville	CI
Donaghenry	Donaghey	Con
Donaghhenry	Stewartstown	PB
Donaghhenry	Donaghenry	Inter
Donaghhenry	St Mary, Stewartstown	RC
Donaghmore	Carland	PB
Donaghmore	Castlecaulfield	PB
Donaghmore	Daughters of the Cross	RC
Donaghmore	Donaghmore (Old)	Inter
Donaghmore	Garvagh Independent	PB
Donaghmore	St John, Galbally	RC
Donaghmore	St Michael, Castlecaulfield	RC
Donaghmore	St Patrick	CI
Donaghmore	St Patrick	RC
Dromore	Church Brae, Dromore	Inter
Dromore	Dromore	PB
Dromore	Holy Trinity, Dromore	CI
Dromore	St Dympna	RC
Dromore	Togherdo	Meth

Civil Parish	Cemetery	Denomination
Drumglass	Convent of Mercy	RC
Drumglass	Coolhill	Inter
Drumglass	Drumcoo, Dungannon	Inter
Drumglass	Drumglass (Old)	RC
Drumglass	St Anne, Dungannon	CI
Drumglass	St Patrick (Old and New)	RC
Drumragh	Clanabogan	CI
Drumragh	Drumragh (Old)	Inter
Drumragh	Dublin Road, Omagh	Inter
Drumragh	Green Hill	Inter
Drumragh	Loreto Convent	RC
Drumragh	Sacred Heart, Omagh	RC
Drumragh	St Mary, Omagh	RC
Errigal Keerogue	Ballynanny	Meth
Errigal Keerogue	St Ciaran, Ballygawley	RC
Errigal Keerogue	St Malachy, Ballymacilroy	RC
Errigal Keerogue	St Mary, Dunmoyle	RC
Errigal Keerogue	St Matthew, Ballynasaggart	CI
Errigal Keerogue	St Matthew, Garvaghy	RC
Errigal Keerogue	Ballygawley	CI
Errigal Keerogue	Ballygawley	PB
Kildress	Kildress (Old)	Inter
Kildress	St Joseph	RC
Kildress	St Mary, Dunamore	RC
Kildress	St Mary, Kildress	RC
Kildress	St Patrick	CI
Killeshill	Clonaneese Upper	PB
Killeshill	St Joseph, Ackinduff	RC
Killeshill	St Joseph, Aughnagar	RC
Killeshill	St Mary, Tullyallen	RC

Civil Parish	Cemetery	Denomination
Killeshill	St Paul, Killeshill	CI
Killyman	Clonmore	RC
Killyman	Mullinakill	Inter
Killyman	St Andrew	CI
Killyman	St Brigid	RC
Kilskerry	Christ Church	CI
Kilskerry	Magheralough	RC
Leckpatrick	Leckpatrick (Old)	Inter
Leckpatrick	St Mary, Cloghcor	RC
Lissan	Claggan	PB
Lissan	Lissan	CI
Lissan	St Michael, Lissan	RC
Longfield West	Drumquin	PB
Longfield West	Lower Langfield, Drumquin	CI
Longfield West	St Mary, Drumquin	RC
Longfield West	St Patrick, Drumquin	RC
Magheracross	St John Baptist, Toura	RC
Pomeroy	Immac Concept, Altmore	RC
Pomeroy	St Mary, Pomeroy	RC
Pomeroy	St Patrick (Old)	RC
Tamlaght	Coagh	PB
Tamlaght	Ss Joseph and Mary, Coagh	RC
Tamlaght	St Luke, Coagh	CI
Termonamongan	Killeter	PB
Termonamongan	Magherakeel	Inter
Termonamongan	St Bestius	CI
Termonamongan	St Patrick, Aughayaran	RC
Termonmaguirk	Sixmilecross	CI
Termonmaguirk	St Mary, Loughmacrory	RC
Termonmaguirk	Drumduff	RC

Civil Parish	Cemetery	Denomination
Termonmaguirk	St Columcille, Carrickmore	CI
Termonmaguirk	St Columcille, Carrickmore	RC
Tullyniskin	Newmills	PB
Tullyniskin	St Malachy, Edendork	RC
Urney	Bridgetown, Castlederg	CI
Urney	St Teresa, Sion Mills	RC
Urney	Urney (Old and New)	Inter